IN WHICH

AND OTHERS
DISCOVER
THE END

T0151889

Published by Plays Inverse Press
Pittsburgh, PA
www.playsinverse.com

ISBN 13: 978-0-9997247-1-2

Cover photo by Theo Goodell
Page and cover design by Tyler Crumrine
Printed in the U.S.A.

IN WHICH

AND OTHERS DISCOVER THE END

RACHEL JENDRZEJEWSKI & SUPERGROUP

Plays Inverse Press
Pittsburgh, PA
2018

on how small structures contribute to the stability of something larger

(a foreword)

Because this text is a score, it asks to be approached by the reader's inner musician: for whom the record of performance-making aims to transcribe a polyphony of tempos, tones, and fugues. Writing sheet music is just another genre of notation using symbols. Similarly, the written score you have here in your hands aims to document fundamentally oral and kinetic practices in order to suspend and arrest, however briefly and provisionally, the breath of living song that is performance. Notation promises that it might not altogether vanish; that performance could be repeatable, if not ever identical, not even by this very same trust of performers. In no particular order, the work is made up of found text, found gesture, and found movement—in addition to the sound, silence, music, original text, and choreography that are also a result of the crew's collaborative findings. Given time, devised work makes composers of us all.

In the aleatory (chance-driven) tradition of sound composition, the partnership between playwright Rachel Jendrzejewski and performance collaborators SuperGroup accommodates a plurality of lyrics, chord progressions, and punctuations, a concert of multiple and simultaneous recitations made of solos, duets, trios, choruses—and so on. To think of performance as an ensemble of singing songwriters (purring, piping, parroting; croaking, crooning, chanting; slurping, slurring; laughing, yelling) affords all participants, including the audience, the chance at what musical notation offers: charting out not just such narrative standards as melody and chord progressions (although these are important tools in any kind of storytelling), but also countermelodies, basslines, embellishments, and improvisational grooves.

Neumatic notation means to facilitate information retrieval: the retention of notes, rhythm, and pitch as well as the remembering of articulation, duration, and tempo. That's what this score means to do as well. On the left page there are notes for movement and choreographic code. On the right page, script. With its letters and phrasings, its spacings on the page communicate the composition's conceptual and organizational interplay through spatial values, collating the topographical with the typographical. Like any score (or script), it's a how-to handbook, a skeleton of action, an instrument waiting to be played. But it's also a caper that doesn't exactly need to be solved. Compulsive in its citationality, the work draws attention to hiccups in the information-processing aspect of found texts (often drawn from digital media sources): accentuating the exercise of notation and retrieval practices (and *systems*), rather than story or "information" itself.

Pay attention to the visual poetry in this score, just as you would pay attention to the ways performers enact not theatrical "characters" on a stage but rather *bodies in space* (a key tenet in post-dramatic theatre). Figure-ground theory says that the space that results from placing figures should be considered as carefully as the figures themselves. The architectural principle is as central to the crafting of theatrical design as it is to devising performance and choreography. In song as in movement, negative and positive shapes emphatically "write" the score. A lot is left unsaid, leaving room for imagination. As leitmotif, the focus on the body is standard fare in the canon of body and performance art, yet no one voice monopolizes authority on the matter, swerving between agency and thing. "Can we keep it focused on the body?" skids off into talk of ligaments in the knee: it has to do with anatomy.

Found gesture, found movement: this is a score generated by rules and chance games, a freeform that is also turned into sequence. Not just an agglomeration of notes (as music theorist Theodor Adorno wryly remarks elsewhere), what the ensemble dares make of it all is what's known as "performance *as* research." Process is all. Often, chance operations in performance contexts reveal the ways in which people slip between objects and subjects of human relations. At root, the technique also brings focus to the ongoing epistemological conundrum (how do we know what we know?) without trying to settle or resolve it. Doubt repeats textually, too—as citational predicament: "The Internet can tell us all the facts" / "I really don't think I know anything at all."

Let us not be fooled by chance operations. In scientific method, where process is also more important than product, it is said that "chance favors only the prepared mind," the one still rigorously open enough to perceive what's right in front of you (Louis Pasteur). The flip side of the control society, chance promises relief from the constraints of rationality (run awry) at the same time that it offers that purer grace: luck. In the interpenetrations of chance and control, it is always better to be lucky. As a matter of method, it is always better to be prepared. Beyond that, who can say?

Navigating the need for homeostasis with that of opportunity, *In Which_____ and Others Discover the End* offers a way of holding out for indeterminacy (and the space of not knowing) in the context of a know-it-all information services economy gnarled with the extremes of abundance, drought, and insolvency—the sorrows of the unlucky, no matter how much practice and preparedness (rehearsal). "I think a lot about the end of the world / I see it coming." On the one hand, the performance quotes conventional apathy, "The problem is that I'm totally disconnected from the Intrnet / my people / geography […] this room could be anywhere / But it's not anywhere." On the other hand, it also cites material wonder: "You are not closed off from the world, but rather are an integral component of it, like a cell in a larger body." The dice are rolling.

The meter and syncopation of chance, change, and quick reaction (improvisation) invent patterns and correlations: vital form. From rhythm, movement, and methexis, story inevitably arises and just as surely recedes—microtonal attractions making connections between instincts for pitch and movement. Eurythmics set off the trials of pathos and the work of repair, one minute to the next. Opening the score, movement codes are cued. "*Emerge into the space / Dance the collective unconscious anxiety that the world may soon become uninhabitable.*" Sometimes there's just the simple directive: "*Generate movement and echo text*" and "*generate text and mimic movement.*" As a body of writing, mimesis and mimicry interplay here in a linguistic kleptomania that appropriates all kinds of discourses from the pandora's box of "lost and found" texts.

As an archive of what happened, formalized for printed presentation, the score can also guide future adaptations. Thinking forward with new makers, it may be helpful to note what is not recorded in the score. For one, the debut performance I saw in northeast Minneapolis

(March 2015) opens with lights flooding the stage in a vigorous saturation of a very particular color: ultraviolet. As a frequency of light (one of the fastest), ultraviolet has its forensic applications. Using it, investigators can "see" otherwise undetectable evidence. In my mind's eye, this work is indelibly coded with the polyphonies of ultraviolet vision, in all its fluorescence.

As color, ultraviolet sits in a relationship of adjacency to the field of purples that are among the most exclusive dyes in history—such as Tyrian purple, made from mucus secreted by the Mediterranean sea snail, murex. Purple of course is royal, liturgical—and popular (see Prince, *Purple Rain*). But as a spectral color, ultraviolet is only transmitted in monochromatic light. Unlike purple, it is mainly visible to insects, mammals, birds, and fish. In effect, the color signals attention to the earthly prevalence of non-human ways of seeing—not an inconsequential detail for a work contemplating the end of things. We are not the only ones facing ruin.

Projecting an ultraviolet deep sea glow over the Liz Miller installation/interactive set stages what could be imagined as patterned seaweeds, suspended from on high. It's funny, because that would make us all underwater creatures, audience and performers alike. Together, the light and the installation suggest a repository of life largely unknown to us *that we are also nevertheless a part of*: watery fathoms that are just as surely a fundament to this earth's survival—to life—as the sun, teeming with life.

At the same time, Miller's installation tinkers between the mechanical and the organic, reminiscent of Donna Haraway's tentacular thinking, between thing and material. It conjures Taylorist leftovers, with the silhouettes of industrial machineries transformed in decorative homage to the romance of warehouse spaces so typical of creatives and creativity rhetorics alike, struggling to get by. Miller's alliterative surfaces dangle and beckon interiority with forms that are defined by economic scarcity, 'silhouette' referring to 18th-century austerity economics that are formally revived in the works of Kara Walker and William Kentridge, too.

Thematically, *In Which _____ and Others Discover the End* offers an approach to the contemporaneity of apocalyptic humors defining the Anthropocene. Earth's eco-systems are in a state of disequilibrium, and time is out of joint. Think the third carbon age, global warming, and the failures of all kinds of social institutions to do anything about it: "If it ends, the blame will be thrown, arms all akimbo." We are no longer fully protected from the ultraviolet rays of electromagnetic radiation. In and of themselves, ultraviolet rays span the range of good and bad chemical and biological effects. As with most things, it is a matter of proportion. Ultraviolet thus sets the stage for the work's apocalyptic wanderings, as matter and as color.

The work I saw also begins in the sonic register, the opening eight minutes punctuated with a hum sounding almost like plainchant melodies, a sound that comes before the formalities of song that eventually brings what seems far (the tonality of early modern music) nearer to compositions of the now. The score says: "*Awaken the voice, almost.*" As an awakening, apparently free-form, it is a patchwork of metered tones, a deep-sea pre-Gregorian chant nicked with the sound of feet dusting the stage, both a random and patterned dispersal of breath and moves. As the light comes up, performers sway in the drift of the tide's constant rhythm.

When it comes, buckle up: Brute Heart's electroacoustic soundscape delivers, cradling interludes of the score's requiem like alluvion in its flow, equal parts everyday babble and epic babel. In the end, there is no sacred. There's rabble. "These are the things we lost / this is what we left behind / these are the things we lost / this is what's left." As chant, such embellishments reveal the throes of that mortal coil Adorno identifies in *Quasi Una Fantasia: Essays on Modern Music*—that wavering between wanting to belong (craving acceptance) and heeding instinctual hostility towards administered society. So while there's plain-talk about the shortcomings of upper Midwest liberalism ("We came. We sat. We ate. We ate dessert."), in Brute Heart's reverb, there's also an echo of the sublime, a deluge of ruination that is also repair.

In the closing 15 minutes, a script is circulated among people in the audience. Some join the stage as part of a growing community of composers: "We help when we can and don't when we can't." "This is what we do." *In Which _____ and Others Discover the End* presents not strategy, per se, but an inquiry into the micropolitics of navigating smaller structures that might sustain the whole—tactics for staying with the "bubble trouble" in ultraviole(n)t worlds. Not your typical Song of Solomon, but there you have it. To riff on Adorno again, wherever polyrhythmic flexibility promises the image of freedom, it must abide the unknowability of what's to come. Rehearsal is no rescue. Friends, hang tight.

Lara D. Nielsen
Almería, Spain

introduction

In 2013, we (SuperGroup and Rachel Jendrzejewski), along with performer-collaborators Angharad Davies, Hannah Kramer, and Stephanie Stoumbelis, made a performance named *it's [all] highly personal (i[a]hp)*. Stemming from conversations with people in our lives about transitional moments and extrapolating out to examine the relationship between ritual and risk, *i[a]hp* was a densely layered, abstract, meditative land-scape. Throughout the development process, we explored the subtle, less obvious shifts (in life, in language, in choreography) that accumulate until you look back and acknowledge a large change. Before long, the subject of death and, in turn, climate change, bubbled up. This led to a lot of discussions about our roles as artist-activists, and how to confront complex social issues in the kind of performance we make without simply becoming didactic. We realized we weren't ready to tackle climate change in *i[a]hp*, so we shelved it, or let it recede, for the time.

Emerging from or through that process, however, the question lingered. As we began our next project together, we realized we weren't finished investigating some of the themes that came up in *i[a]hp*; and we were compelled to circle back to the particularly huge, slow, unimaginable shifts of climate change. As we began work on *In Which _____ and Others Discover the End*, we spent time examining the difficulties that had been coming up for us surrounding climate change and performance. We generated a list like this: the hugeness of the scale, the slow burn effects, the overwhelming-ness, the deluge of information, the inevitability, all the other performances that were addressing it. Through discussions amongst ourselves and by reading the work of folks like Joanna Macy, a scholar of ecology and Buddhism, we started to make a relational comparison: death is to climate change as the individual body is to the body of the collective. What if, in this piece, our wrestling with climate change is less informational or representational, and is instead experiential? What if our goal is not to provide solutions, is not a call to action, is not a cathartic encounter, but instead is an attempt at the embodiment of our collective unconscious, of our collective body? *In Which _____ and Others Discover the End* is about climate change, but it's also about transitions and binaries and death and community. It is about the people in the room who made it, and it is about the people in the room who are experiencing it together.

Over the course of two years, together with our collaborators, we followed a non-linear creation path marked by the loose exchange of ideas, sound and movement scores, found texts, script pages, shades of blue, choreography, and many, many emails. Information was cycled, and recycled, through the various domains of the process: our focus on the body, voice, language, and structural dramaturgy in dialogue with performers Stephanie, Angharad, and Hannah; Brute Heart's instrumental sonic landscape; Liz Miller's visual object landscape; and Hannah Geil-Neufeld's "process correspondence" work, which invited the audience into the fold long before and after the project was presented to the public.

In Which _____ and Others Discover the End came to fruition in March/April 2015 at Public Functionary, a contemporary art and social space in Minneapolis, thanks in no small part to its risk-taking, visionary directors Tricia Heuring and Mike Bishop. The project was framed in four parts, all open to the public free of charge: an exhibition of Liz's immersive visual installation, several weeks of open rehearsals, a series of "take-over" events curated by Public Functionary happening amidst the installation, and a culminating run of live performances—from which the book you are holding has been drawn.

For this publication, by invitation and with so much thoughtful care from editor Tyler Crumrine, we are walking the fine lines between archive, literature, and working script—a book that notates, after the fact, what happened in the original collaboration; a book that could be read without ever seeing a performance; and a book that offers an evocative guide for potential future stagings by others. Toward these latter ends, we've maintained a deliberate spaciousness in our notes about choreography and staging, in order to allow for the varied imaginations, associations, and contributions of readers and other artists. The illustrations throughout the book are adapted from images taken of the premiere by Theo Goodell and Joe and Jen Photography, documentation re-membered or imagined. The two pieces of music included in the back of the book (two pieces we composed outside of the Brute Heart sound score) serve a similar purpose—a remnant of what was: a possibility of what could be, albeit unguaranteed.

Rachel Jendrzejewski & SuperGroup
Minneapolis, MN

performance history

In Which _____ *and Others Discover the End* began as a multi-phase project, with a culminating performance run, that unfolded over five weeks during March and April 2015 at Public Functionary (Co-Directors Tricia Heuring and Mike Bishop) in Minneapolis, MN. It included a visual installation by Liz Miller, original music created and performed live by Brute Heart (Crystal Brinkman, Jackie Beckey, and Crystal Myslajek), and lighting designed by Heidi Eckwall. Sound Engineer: Kevin Springer. Board Op: Eric Larson. Process Correspondent: Hannah Geil-Neufeld.

The performers were as follows:

A	Angharad Davies
E	Erin Search-Wells
H	Hannah Kramer
J	Jeffrey Wells
R	Rachel Jendrzejewski
S	Sam Johnson
ST	Stephanie Stoumbelis

The creation and premiere of *In Which* _____ *and Others Discover the End* was made possible by Public Functionary, The Jerome Foundation, Carleton College, Marcy Open School, University of Minnesota's Institute for Advanced Study, The Playwrights' Center, 61 individual donors, 300+ audience members, and the voters of Minnesota through a grant from the Metropolitan Regional Arts Council thanks to a legislative appropriation from the Arts and Cultural Heritage Fund.

reading this book

Bold text indicates section headings for easy reference. *Italics* indicate stage directions. ***Bold italics*** indicate singing.

The left page is a physical score (prompts for movement). The right page is a vocal score (including both text and vocal affects). Of course, speaking and singing are also physical acts, so please move freely between the two sections as you read. These scores have been aligned with intention, toward approximating the timing of their overlaps, but there is also plenty of wiggle room for allowing sections to take as long as they need. Stretches of silence are appropriate. When tasks are not assigned to specific performers, everyone available participates.

This performance is intended for a relatively intimate space with no "off-stage" area. The cast is in the space at all times, though may be occupying the periphery, including in and around the audience.

The original collaboration's full music score by Brute Heart and immersive visual installation by Liz Miller were vital to the live experience of the work. For future performances, we ask artists to holistically consider your own approach to sound and visual environment hand in hand with this script.

Before the performance begins, J, H, R, and ST each should gather a group of audience members and assign them roles for Part 3, corresponding to their respective numbers in the script (e.g. J assigns audience members 1a, 1b, 1c, 1d, 1e, 1f, 1g, and 1h).

For Iris, Henry, and Alma
(babies, babies, babies)

"Until the late twentieth century, every generation throughout history lived with the tacit certainty that there would be generations to follow. Each assumed, without questioning, that its children and children's children would walk the same Earth, under the same sky. Hardships, failures, and personal death were encompassed in that vaster assurance of continuity. That certainty is now lost to us, whatever our politics. That loss, unmeasured and immeasurable, is the pivotal psychological reality of our time."

—Joanna Macy
Working Through Environmental Despair

"…where is it that we can gather and kind of be alone together? And, you know, there's so much, as we all know, 'us/them.' And what are the circumstances for 'we,' that I can enjoy the pleasure of something I'm seeing here, knowing that I'm also sharing that with a person next to me? And there's an interesting kind of intimacy with this total stranger that the situation makes possible."

—Ann Hamilton, interview with Krista Tippett
On Being: Making, and the Spaces We Share

PART 1

JJ
Emerge into the space.

Dance the collective unconscious anxiety that the world may soon become uninhabitable.

Create an internal engine.

Relate as performers.

Islands
Spill forth the inner impossible tasks of the body and engage in the inner impossible tasks of others' bodies.

Interplay between internal and external.

Shift the focus through space.

This is as precious as it is but not more precious.

Walking between islands is a direct, known movement; a task.

Therapy 1
Walking between islands shifts casual, like when you are at someone's house sitting at a kitchen counter and they are cooking or cleaning or something.

PART 1

Developmental Vocal Score
Awaken the voice, almost.

Use some sort of logic, some sort of progression.

Closed to open, soft to hard, long to short, simple to complex.

Become, together, a shifting landscape of dissonance and resolution.

Therapy 1
The voices are malleable, continuously slipping into different qualities. There is nothing forced or calculated. Vocal changes are the result of physical and sonic association. The voices take turns shifting away and modulating toward each other.

A

I wonder if my discomfort is related to my comfort.

E

I wonder if my comfort is related to my discomfort.

A

I wonder if that's true.

E

I mean I wonder if anything's true.

A

Hey, we're just talking. Old school style.

E

I mean I think part of the problem is that
I'm totally disconnected from the Internet.
I can't get any kind of signal in here.
Is there a hidden one?

A

No.

E

What's the name of your signal then?
Is there a password?

A

No.

E

No signal or no password?
Because you should really password protect.

A

Is protection important to you?

E

I mean I think part of the problem is that
I'm totally disconnected from my people.

A

You were saying?

E

When? I wasn't really saying anything.

A

Your people.

E

I mean I think part of the problem is that
I'm totally disconnected from my geography.
I'm not from here.
This room could be anywhere.

A

But it's not anywhere.

E

I mean I think part of the problem is that
I'm totally disconnected from my body.

A

Oh! Well that sounds quite promising.
Can you say more about that?

E

Well. Sometimes actually a lot of times,

I go through my days feeling like
my eyes are looking into, I don't know,
a computer screen
or some kind of electronic device, I mean
even when I'm not actually looking at one,
and I find myself feeling like
I'm moving through it, into it.
But meanwhile my actual body is just,
there, here, wherever that is, you know,
hanging like a damp towel.

A
Hanging like a damp towel.

E
What is it doing? I really honestly have no idea.

A
Well let's explore!
Why don't you try tuning into your body right now.
What is it doing?

E
uhhhhhhhhhhhh

A
Excuse me?

E
I have no idea.

A
You can take a minute to tune in. Listen.

E

Quite frankly, it's not my job to know my body.
I'm not a doctor or a PE teacher.
Don't we pay those people to know things
about the body?
I just sit in front of a computer all day. That's my work.
My body's pretty irrelevant in that work.

A

What specifically do you do?

E

I know a lot about computers.

A

But what specifically do you do?

E

Oh all kinds of things. In front of computers.

A

Okay. But using your body.
I mean you have to use your body to use the computer.
Your body uses the computer.

E

I mean I guess so. Barely. It seems like barely.
But sometimes I wonder, do I?

A

Do you what—have a body?

E

Well you just told me I have a body.

A

Well but do you think so?

E

Well I was there.

A

Were you?

E

What?

A

What?

E

Who?

A

Let's go back a bit.
What I wanted to ask is—
do you need to have a professional focus on the body
to know your body?
Actually what I wanted to ask is—
who am I in relation to others?
Actually what I really wanted to ask is—
where can I find yesterday's weather forecasts?
I'm sorry, what I wanted to ask is—
doesn't everyone have a body?

E

Not everyone.

A

Well, okay.

Tell me more about how it feels
to be disconnected from your body.

E

Uhh… Sometimes, or actually a lot of times,
I go through the days feeling like
my legs are big tree trunks,
just kind of rolling around from place to place.
I feel very clunky.

A

Well, that's normal.

E

Is it? Should it be?
I think that's a big part of my concern.
How many normal things "should" feel normal
like they really are actually normal and good
and we should all accept them
and talk about them more,
versus how many normal things are actually
really terrible messed up things
that are not actually normal
but that we've all, for some reason,
agreed are normal?

A

Mmmm.
Can you think of some other examples
of things we've all agreed are normal
that perhaps should not be normal?

E

I can think of so many things. Marketing. Debt. Cars.

A

Can we keep it focused on the body?

E

Those things have everything to do with the body.

A

Let's focus on the present.
What is your body doing right now?

E

It's like it's not even there.
If it begins someplace, I don't know where.
If it ends, the blame will be thrown, arms all akimbo.
By then, innards will have been coal for decades,
cancer quite normal I suppose.

A

Excuse me?

E

I'm focusing on the future now.

A

Okay.

E

Our biological makeup will be all different.
The past present participle is a tough one to make real.
It implies the ability, in the present,
to still affect the future.
It has no permanence, only possible repercussions,
a long list of them.
So our bodies might be stiffer.

A

Or should we imagine a better option where
they are pliable and accustomed to wetness?
Will there be an underwater world?

E

But it's a given and we must be we.
We must admit it together and then
dance about it like a bunch of hippies.
Like Burning Man. If Burning Man worked.
If energy could work.

A

If harnessing human energy was possible.

E

Would movements spark up to say it is inhumane?
The inability to cause anything.
To work for a cause because.
A beastly burden.

A

That's common, that phrase.

E

Still parties, a spaceship probe.
No plans for a real end.

A

Billions of people sleep at the same time.

E

Babies babies babies.

J: cross through the space and exit.

Interpreter/Conversation Loop
During E's story, ST enters (from behind the audience, eventually arriving on stage), followed by R, and then J.

All four performers are occupied by simultaneous tasks:
E: generate text and mimic ST's movement.
ST: generate movement and echo J's text.

A and E

A split in the plan. Motion toward centers,
ways groups form, approaching another group.
What is different about smiling?
Choose to ignore pain or balance.
Feel heaviness and tie it to inevitableness.
Like a beast thrashing blindly.
Investigate the immediate perimeter
and reachable space around and under
the legs which serve as anchors.
Fear of giving too much over to weight.
Splitting hairs, back and forth, swinging
hands like cranes, racing words.
The bottoms of feet are more stable,
hands hurt quicker than feet, placing weight
in controlled measures, never looking around
but being very aware of others.

E

It's annoying that men keep walking through here.

A

I'm glad it wasn't while I was gyrating.

J

Hey E, will you tell that story about [the first time you
went to Italy*]?

Interpreter/Conversation Loop

*E: improvise the telling of a story; one of those stock stories
that you tell over and over. Or learn and use this one.*

J: periodically ask questions.

R: generate movement and echo E's text.
J: generate text and mimic R's movement.

ST: emphatically, unequivocally, physically
state your joy story and defend it from all attacks.
R: physically converse with ST, derailing their story.

All: navigate the disparate tasks at hand.

E

Oh the first time I went to Italy? It was the only time I went to Italy. I don't go to Italy all the time. But it was um, college, and it was um, spring break, um, 2002, and um, I was really too young to fully appreciate Rome. At all. 'Cause I treated it like, like Spring Break. So I drank wine and I partied, and my mom's in the audience so I won't go into full detail.

But basically the story is actually none of that, the story is the first, um, day that I arrived my friend Kate and I like rushed around and saw a billion old things, I don't even remember what they were, like really important things. And then I was like I'm gonna die because I'm jet lagged and I have to go back to your apartment to take a nap.

So I was overly tired and I laid down in her bed in the dark room and as I was trying to fall asleep suddenly I felt like, ah, this presence and I saw the doorknob slowly opening and the door opened and I saw these, like, four small ghostly female figures. Very short, see-through, and white. And they were wearing like robes, and they were whispering to each other and going *(whispered gibberish)*, and it was maybe in another language, maybe Italian… And they were going *(whispered gibberish)*. And then suddenly I could hear them whisper "Safe Now. Watch over you." And I was petrified. Even though it was a good message I was like oh my god, this is a ghost, these are ghosts, I'm being visited by ghosts. And I was so scared. Um, and I finally got up—

J

When you say they were white, do you mean like Caucasian or—

E
No…

J
—like white like a ghost?

E
No! Like a ghost. They looked exactly like ghosts in movies.

J
Like cartoon ghosts?

E
Mmm, well.

J
Or more like Ghost Dad?

E
More like Jim Henson's Creature Shop ghosts.

J
I've never seen that so I don't know that reference.

E
You know in Muppet Christmas Carol—

J
Okay.

E
When they are—when the ghosts of Christmas Past, maybe? The little doll that's see-through and she flies through the air?

J

Uh huh. But they looked like real people, not
Muppets…

E

They looked exactly like La Pietà, which I had seen that
day. And later I learned about lucid dreaming, which is
what it was.

J

What was the bed like?

E

Oh, just like a dorm bed.

J

I always picture like a big giant wooden old bed.

E

Like a ghost bed?

J

Yeah.

E

Yeah.

J

Well, I don't know what a ghost bed is.

E

Yeah, like an old bed.

J

Um, do you believe in ghosts?

Circumstance Lanes
S, A, ST, and H.

Inhabit the infinite, specific possibilities of your body under other circumstances.

Focus on the real / imagined world around you.

E

Well, here's the thing, I don't. But I'm kind of afraid to say I don't believe in ghosts in case the ghosts get upset about that.

J

But mostly you don't believe.

E

Yes.

J

I was just reading that—I was just reading on the back of a Chipotle bag—

E

Uh huh?

J

—that 58 percent of people—I don't know if that's people in the world or America—um, don't believe in ghosts. So that means—

E

Probably just America.

J

What's that?

E

Probably just America.

J

Probably just America. You think? Why?

E
Did Chipotle do a poll?

J
No, it was actually a short writing by Amy Tan!

E
Oh! Ho ho.

J
But apparently Amy Tan believes in ghosts, but her husband doesn't.

Things We Lost 1
Progress from private contemplation to public declaration.

ST
these are the things we lost
this is what we left behind
these are the things we lost
this is what's left
these are the things and moments and people
some of these are good things
these are left behind
these are the things that we have lost
these are the things we lost
this is what's left
these are the things we lost
this is what's left
only rights are left
some of these are good things
some things are left
these are the things and moments and people
these are left behind
these are the things we judge to be good or not good

Cosmonauts
Anchors and orbits.

Frame the other.

Get it done.

Famous Walks
Find yourself on display.

Focus out past the audience.

Scale the celebrity of your imagination; scale your visibility.

Up/Down
Share in a communal experience of landscape, of vistas, of stillness, of indecision.

Allow shifting roles in shifting dramas.

Allow the gaze to rest on things: objects / performers / audience.

these are the things we judge
these are the things and moments and people
this is what's left
these are the things we lost
some things are left
these are the things we lost
this is what we judge to be good or not good
these are what we judge to be bad
these are the things and moments and people
some of these are good things
some of these are judged to be good things
While this is a "rediscovery"

*Nonverbal space while **Cosmonauts**, **Famous Walks**, and **Up/Down** continue.*

Things We Lost 2
ST
this is what's left
this is what's right
we should pass on the right
we should pass on the right
some of these are good things
some things are left
these are the things and moments and people

While this is a "rediscovery"
these are left behind
these are the things we judge to be good or not good
these are what we judge to be bad
these are what we judge to be bad
While this is a "rediscovery"
some of these are good things
this is what's left
these are the things we lost
some of these are bad things
this is what's left
this is what's left
some of these are good things
some things are left
these are the things and moments and people
While this is a "rediscovery"
these are left behind
these are the things we judge to be good or not good
these are what we judge to be bad
these are what we judge to be bad
some of these are good things
this is what's left
only rights are left
these are the things we lost
some of these are bad things

Knee Conversation 1[1]

Convivially argumentative.

ST

For example: if current medical science
can miss something as simple as a knee ligament,
just think how much we are still in the Stone Age
when it comes to something as complex as
the human brain.

Someday we will look back on today's
mental health treatments and say
"how barbaric."

H
While this is a "rediscovery"
of the ligament that the Doctor reconstructed,
it is always important to re-evaluate previous work.

S
Yes, it is no small task.

H
In most patients, the A-L-L is a thin layer of tissue
which becomes tightened only when
the knee is internally rotated.

S
Many peers contacted me for more information
after the news was announced.

ST
Anatomists live for this sort of thing.
Everything old is new again.
I see this kind of thing all the time at my job.

J
No single scientific paper constitutes
real understanding of anything.

H
Would any scientist ever claim otherwise?
I quote: "If we knew what we were doing,
it wouldn't be called 'research.'"

E Solo
Begin the mourning process.

R

This is so great! We can have a new diagnosis!

ST

Actually quite a few body parts have been discovered
in recent years.

E

Yeah. Great.
Another piece of tissue to be treated
for thousands of dollars.
Just what the doctor ordered.

J

I'm with you.
So after a gazillion autopsies
and a gazillion prints of Grey's Anatomy,
they've found a new ligament.

E

Now if only I could pay for the soon to be needed care
with bitcoin!

ST

Ignorance is not bliss.

*Nonverbal space while **E Solo** continues.*

Individuals

Assert communicative joy in movement, describing the poetically transitional nature of relationships, of lives, of bodies.

Allow an active presence.

Take in each other as each other.

Knee Conversation 2
Heated, loud.

E
There is no understanding of the importance
of gathering data over long periods of time.

R
No understanding of the length of time
and number of studies it takes for proof to be conclusive.

E
Totally. We now know that earth orbits the sun.
There was a time when it would be a death sentence
to prove otherwise.

R
There was a time when the world was thought to be flat.

E
I imagine a sentiment expressed at the time
might have been,
"Any fool can see that the world is flat. Look at my field."

S
The important part of this "discovery" is how
this small structure contributes to
stability of a large joint.

J
It's ridiculous that they did not know
about this ligament!
For God's sake, you can feel it with your fingers!

ST
I felt it for years,
mainly due to various injuries in my legs due to running.
People, stay away from running.

S
Sorry, you're wrong. "Stay away from running?" Really?

H
So, those paleolithic humans should not have run
with their spear to kill the bison so they can eat?

S
They shouldn't run away from the animal
that is chasing them?
Just walk, right?

H
Walk and hope.

S
I don't know what your background is, but
from what you say, I can't imagine you're very good
at giving the appropriate advice.

E
Bones and muscle are muscles and bones.

H
The important part of this "discovery" is how
this small structure contributes to
stability of a large joint.

J
A good proportion of us have studied anatomy—

just of the chicken.

ST
Dissecting a human knee is an activity
not completely separate from deboning a chicken.

E
Bones and muscle are muscles and bones.

J
I am stupefied by this discovery.
What an embarrassing discovery—and congratulations.

S
This is absolutely amazing! It is as if mathematicians
had found a new whole number between nine and ten.

H
Actually, it's nothing at all like that.
It's a descriptive anatomical issue.

ST
This is absolutely amazing! It is as if mathematicians
had found a new whole number between nine and ten.

H
Actually, it's nothing at all like that.
It's a descriptive anatomical issue.

R
This is absolutely amazing! It is as if mathematicians
had found a new whole number between nine and ten.

E
Bones and muscle are muscles and bones.

ST Gets Dressed

Test the image of representation, play the socially engaged body.

ST Gets Dressed[2]
ST
Thank you!
Great to be here!
Very interesting and unique!
Deep!
Good!
Awesome!
Beautiful!
Fantastic!
Impressive!
Hypnotic and impressive!
Beautiful work!
Great job!
Great!
SO GREAT!
Wow!
Nice job!
Totally captivating!
Spectacular!
Quite wonderful!
Original!
Amazing!
Absolutely amazing!
Interesting!
Fun!
Emotional!
Moving!
Fun!
Thought-provoking!
Hypnotic!
Long!
Extremely full!
Provocative!
This made the list!

You make my day!
beauty
harmony
church choir
execution
machine
personality
restraint
planning
catharsis
catharsis
Some parts made me sad
distracted
bored
there was a very lulling quality.
It also called my attention to
my desire for continuity,
synchronization
connectivity.
I felt a certain degree of anxiety
when things didn't follow
the pattern I expected.
overstimulating
overwhelming
Something similar in the 60s
one heck of a lot better
Love me some repetition!
LOVED! Love it!
Wish my 6-year-old son was here.
totally extraneous movement
not connected to anything
stayed the same throughout
voice thing is old
tedious
I hate Philip Glass.

You/No 1
ST: dance the text.

You are subject and object.

Allow for play.

Allow for embarrassment.

Allow for obviousness.

I found certain parts relevant to my life
and other parts boring
what impresses also irritates
Point made about blah
Point made about the relentless cacophony of humanity
Purposefully self-absorbed statements
Rises to a Babel-like level
delivered and repeated
and repeated
and repeated
and repeated
and repeated
Babies babies babies
and repeated
and repeated
and repeated
and repeated
and repeated
and repeated
and repeated
and repeated

You/No 1³
R: read from a script behind the audience.

R
You are clever but uncontrollable.
You cast away your fanatical deliberation
of the conditions that have defined your life.
You exchange them for an earnest, if sometimes tedious,
absorption with the affliction of someone else:
the pummeled, besieged old Mother Nature.
You ask, "Is this the way Earth will end,
or at least our presence on it?"
You present hilariously dismal words

Physical Ostinato

Lose yourself in task.

Allow relationship to 'Pop Song' to play

and repeat it
and repeat it
and repeat it.

about the deteriorating state of the planet
and its inhabitants—
bleak missives about the extinction of species,
ocean acidification,
and the futility of global climate meetings
turned cheerful and postmodern.
You pack dense arsenals of information about
humanity's abuse of the environment
into a lurid tale of an inexplicable disappearance.
This approach is unconventional for you.
You say,
"This is how I am carving out a path,
or digging a tunnel, or stringing a line
between my former narcissistic reality
and a broader sphere of compassion."
You've been on CNN like nine times.

How We Survive
J and R
This is how we survive day to day
It's how we survive
Discover god by the railroad tracks
Understand god as human contact
The ways in which we find meaning
Like nose blowing
Like skirt pinning

Pop Song
J and ST: lead.
A, E, H, R, and S: back up.

Indulge and surrender to pop cheese.

J and R
I love this or I'm good at this

ALL
I love this or I'm good at this
I love this or I'm good at this
I love this or I'm good at this
I love this

J and ST
A split in the plan
Motion towards centers
Ways groups form
Approaching another group
What is different about smiling
Choose to ignore pain or balance
Feel heaviness and tie it to inevitableness
Like a beast thrashing blindly
Investigate the immediate perimeter
And reachable space
Around and under the legs
Which serve as anchors
Under the legs
Which serve as anchors

A, E, S, and ST
I love this I love this I love

J
There is a springtime fullness
There is running in the fields
Those smells like grass and floral blooms

ALL
General and specific

J and ST
There is blood and movement and rush

An energy
Zip zap pulse pulse pulse
Maximum capacity
Maximum output
Maximum capacity
Maximum output

H and R
I see it coming
I see it coming
I see it coming
I see it coming

A, E, and S
It's coming coming
coming coming
coming coming
coming coming

A, E, H, R, and S
I love this

J and ST
Splitting hairs, back and forth
Swinging hands like cranes

A, E, H, R, and S
I love this

J and ST
Racing words
The bottoms of feet are more stable, hands

A, E, H, R, and S
I love this

Circumstance Clump
Discover the myriad of interlocking selves that can create "community" or maybe that is gross.

J and ST
Hurt quicker than feet
Placing weight in controlled measures
Never looking around but being very
Aware of others

ALL
I love this or I'm good at this
I love this or I'm good at this
I love this or I'm good at this
I love this
I love this

J
I think a lot about the end of the world.

Comfort/Discomfort
The following section is improvised.
Use these or other invented lines starting with
"I wonder if my comfort is related to…" and
"I wonder if my discomfort is related to…"
The order, timing, and number of lines spoken also are
improvised. Overlapping is fine.
Moments of silence are also fine.

H: make a choice about when to return to scripted
language.

I wonder if my discomfort is related to the intelligence of
    my body
I wonder if my comfort is related to dissonance
I wonder if my comfort is related to that new chef-driven
    restaurant
I wonder if my discomfort is related to my gender
    identity

J

Ah—well, I don't know.

It doesn't feel worth regurgitating a lot of facts,

you know?

The Internet can tell us all the facts we need to know.

R

It can?

J

Yeah—

H

That's amazing.

J

I guess.

R

What were you saying?

J

Just that—

It's more this feeling that there might be only

one or two generations after me.

If any after me.

Like in my family.

R

You don't want kids?

J

No, I mean—because of the world ending.

H
You don't want kids because the world is ending?

J
No, that's not what I mean.
Whether or not I want them,
it's the fact the world is ending.

R
Right now?

J
Not this minute—per se—but soon.
Within one or two generations after me.
What with the, you know, the climate.
And all.

R
That seems pretty soon.

J
Too soon?

H
Oh, far too soon I'd say.
That's quite the exaggeration, I'd say.

J
Well it could be that soon.
It really might be that soon.
At the rate things are going.

R
Well it could be. It might be.

J
Even if it's three or four generations after me.
It's this knowledge that maybe that's it.
No more descendants.
Or just you know, people in my family.
Lineage. Continuing on.

R
But you really never know.

J
No, you really never know, but all signs point to—

R
Do you know?

J
No, of course not.

R
I know.

J
Know what?

H
What?

J
Do you know?

R
Know what?

Duet

A and H dance a unison-ish dance.

Give in to something else—form, unison, each other.

Sink into procedural knowledge.

Exist in the space.

Herald the coming storm.

J

I really don't think I know anything at all.

R

I know anything at all.
Ask me anything.
Anything at all.

J

There are theories, you know,
about how we're carrying all this knowledge around,
carrying this knowledge around with us
in our bodies
every day.

H

I know. Ask me anything.

J

Where is it, exactly?

R

The knowledge?

J

Yeah.

H

Can we keep it focused on the body?

J

Isn't it in the body?

R

Is it or isn't it?

J

Do you know about the anterolateral ligament?
In the knee. Nobody knew it was there until recently.
How did we not know it was there?
Isn't it right there in view when people dissect the knee?
How did we not know it was there?

R

Let's focus on the present.
What is your body doing right now?

J

I don't know.

H

Why not?

*Nonverbal space while **Duet** continues.*

PART 2

Walking
A: walk.
Find frustration, satisfaction, joy, and sorrow in precision,
in specificity, in simplicity.

S: join the walking.

A: drop out.
S: continue.

PART 2

It's All Highly Personal
A
it's all highly personal
it's all highly general
it's all highly generally shared
you're all personally responsible

S and A
we're all generally responsible
we're all generally personable

S
it's all highly personal
it's all generally highly personal
we're personally responsible
you're personally general
it's all very highly worldwide
yet personal
yet local
we're all personally responsible
which is general
which is personal
which is responsible
which is false
worldwide general
highly worldwide
highly local
highly personal ripple effect
you're worldwide
you're generally local
you're responsibly general
general hospital
you're responsibly worldwide

H: enter and join the walking.

yet personable
personal
shared
you're personally responsible
I'm highly general
you're all highly personal
we're all generally personable
all local
all responsible
all general
all false

S and H
highly general ripple effect
your responsible ripple
your general person
it's that kind of small town
it's that kind of small local
it's that ripple bubble
it's that general ripple
which is personal
which is responsible
which is worldwide
which is false
but shared
it's that kind of small worldwide ripple
it's that kind of bubble trouble
it's general
it's local
it's highly personal
it's highly responsible
which is personal
which is worldwide
which is general
general hospital

S: drop out and exit.

Circumstance Set
*H, J, S, and ST: relive your other imaginary selves,
in relation to the reliving of the group.*

Eventually the reliving turns to something shared.

which is ripple trouble
which is shared
it's all highly personal but shared
it's all highly generally shared
it's highly personal
it's generally local

H
we're personally responsible
you're personably general
it's all very highly worldwide
which is responsible
which is general
which is personal
which is false
generally worldwide
highly general
highly worldwide
highly local personal ripple effect
yet personable
yet shared, because
you're all highly personal
all local
all general
all ripple
all false
highly personal ripple effect
our shared ripple
your general personal
it's that kind of small town
it's that bubble ripple

H and J
which is false
which is worldwide

Quintet

H, J, R, S, and ST: ramp up the physical self,
reinvestigate representation, wear down.
Continue. Disrupt. Fail. Exhaust.

*For **Quintet** the following four movement sections are*
performed mashed together and layered on top of each other.
*The section should end with everyone in **Running**.*

Cosmonauts (reprise)

Individuals (reprise)

Folk Dance

Dance on the counts. It's a one, two, three, four. It's a circle
you can leave and return to, but it dances like an eternal
flame.

Running

Like a pack of animals, of joy, of athletes.

which is personal
which is responsible
but shared
it's that kind of bubble
trouble
it's that kind of small worldwide
it's global
it's general
it's personal
it's shared

*Nonverbal space while **Circumstance Set** continues and **Quintet** begins.*

Cacophony
The following individual scores are yelled/sung swiftly, simultaneously.

Individual Score: J
we are apart
we are together
both and back outside

I wonder if my comfort is related to the weather.
I wonder if my comfort is related to my bed.
I wonder if my comfort is related to celebrity mishaps.
I wonder if my comfort is related to my tax bracket.
I wonder if my comfort is related to my neighborhood.
A tiny Dixie cup over the head.
Just let them be kids.

Individual Score: H
There is a springtime fullness.
There is running in fields.
Those smells like grass and floral blooms—
general and specific.
There is blood and movement and rush.
An energy—zip zap pulse pulse pulse
firing on all of those cylinders.
Running and jumping and recognizing each other.
Here are rotators, a density.
Maximum capacity.
Maximum output.
I see it coming.
I see spring back there, back there.
I see spring ahead.
Some kind of stillness at the center of it.

Individual Score: A
I wonder if my comfort is decreasing as time passes.
I wonder if my comfort will get harder to attain.
I wonder if my comfort is a gift.
I wonder if my comfort can be given away.

we are apart
we are together

Time. Energy. Resources.
Acknowledgment. Credit given.
The reality of money that sometimes stares us down.
The actual position of not having enough food to eat
or a healthy place to live.
A state of mind. And a physical state.

Individual Score: ST
these are the things we lost
this is what's left
these are the things we lost
this is what's left
some of these are good things

it is this relationship
this relationship

Knee surgeons have found a new knee ligament,
one that had not been identified before,
despite thousands upon thousands
of past knee dissections and scans.

Individual Score: S
In the years thereafter,
its existence was forgotten or overlooked or ignored.
This development should improve
our knowledge of how the knee works
and why some knee surgeries don't work out.

we are apart
we are together
we are apart

we are together

Some patients were having a mysterious problem.
While their treated knees appeared to be healthy,
the joint would sometimes buckle as they moved.

Individual Score: R
these are the things we lost
this is what we left behind
these are the things we lost
this is what's left
these are the things and moments and people
these are the things we judge to be good or not good
Shit happens all the time.
New people, new life,
being born all the time.
Babies, babies, babies.
How will you cope with problems?
Do what's best or not best.
Just let them be kids.
Make a difference.
What the hell does that mean?
Did I miss something?

Individual Score: E⁴
"That certainty is now lost to us, whatever our politics…
What we are really dealing with here
is akin to the original meaning of compassion…
It is inseparable from the currents of
matter, energy, and information
that flow through us and sustain us
as interconnected open systems."

like nose blowing
like skirt pinning

"We are not closed off from the world,
but rather are integral components of it,
like cells in a larger body."

PART 3

You/No Stories
Dance the text.

Starts with A on stage; others enter throughout the section.

You are subject and object.

Allow for play.

Allow for embarrassment.

Allow for obviousness.

Find aggressive engagement in the ridiculous, in the simplistic, in the apathetic smallness, in the futility, in the pleasure of being here with other bodies.

Remembering that this is for/with an audience.

Remembering that you can get lost in the imaginative worlds that the text brings up, describing not just the object but also the surroundings, etc...

PART 3

You/No 2[5]
J: read 1 from a script behind the audience.

1

You are clever but uncontrollable.
You cast away your fanatical deliberation
of the conditions that have defined your life.
You exchange them for an earnest, if sometimes tedious,
absorption with the affliction of someone else:
the pummeled, besieged old Mother Nature.
You ask, "Is this the way the Earth will end,
or at least our presence on it?"
You present hilariously dismal words
about the deteriorating state of the planet
and its inhabitants—
bleak missives about the extinction of species,
ocean acidification,
and the futility of global climate meetings
turned cheerful and postmodern.
You pack dense arsenals of information about
humanity's abuse of the environment
into a lurid tale of an inexplicable disappearance.
This approach is unconventional for you.
You say,
"This is how I am carving out a path,
or digging a tunnel, or stringing a line
between my former narcissistic reality
and a broader sphere of compassion."
You've been on CNN like nine times.

H: read 2 from a script behind the audience.

E: join movement.

2

No, you've been on <u>ABC</u> like nine times.

1

You are trying to tell a story with no chance of success.
You say, "The problem with climate change is
things can happen in one place that impact people
in a totally different place, and even a different time."

2

You've started to feel that even adorable children
sounding distress signals about the poor planet
have lost their endearment in our incessantly
scrolling sphere.

1

You sound a distress signal that
you have to know is familiar to us.

2

You have to know we have a penchant for the unknown.

1

You have to know we're already well aware
of our carbon footprint.

2

You have to know most of us here are against fracking.

1

You are sometimes didactic.

2

Yet whenever you start to get didactic,
something changes and startles.

S: join movement.

R: read 3 from a script behind the audience.

3
No, your "inquiry" mostly feels like a hokey lead-up to
your sermon.

1
No, you tuned in to these problems
ahead of everyone else…

3
No. You mean well and everything you say is true,
but these nevertheless feel like lessons we've already
learned. It's boring.

1
You point out with painful clarity that
we are swiftly making this planet uninhabitable
for the "we" of the very near future.
It's desperately time-sensitive.

3
You underline your point repeatedly
as a blizzard buries the East Coast.
Okay, we get it. Got it. Point taken.

2
You capture my attention,
as do the melting ice caps and polar bears.
You are witty and vivid.
But over time, you get off track.
You create more awareness around a hot-button issue,
but your approach is anticlimactic.
You don't meet my expectations.

J: pass script to audience member 1a. Join movement.

H: pass script to audience member 2a. Join movement.

1

Your expectations are wrong.

3

YOU yourself are the focus.
You are pervasive and vulnerable, but also absent.
You reduce, reuse, recycle a time-honored work
into your own composition.

2

You collect imagery of wild wonder; it's seductive.

3

You wonder if your discomfort is related to seduction.

2

You find cheeky charm in mesmerizing megafauna.

3

You let urgent topics whiz by:
the melting of ice caps.
The starvation of polar bears.

2

But you unpack the reactions
that climate change provokes in people:
repudiation, complacency, exhaustion,
dawdling, lies, frustration.

1a

You are charged with the difficult job of
advancing the action.

3

You move in response to the words people are saying.

R: pass script to audience member 3a. Join movement.

1a: pass script to audience member 1b.

3a: pass script to audience member 3b.

1a

You look like a glamorous woodland being
and vocalize with a youthful lilt.

3

You get a rise out of us with your impression of
a visitor from outer space
disguised as a man with a moustache.

2a

No, disguised as a <u>woman</u> with a moustache.

ST: read 4 from a script behind the audience.

4

No, disguised as a <u>person with a beard</u>.

1a

You are an ambitious glacial geologist,
eager to get moving on your research.

3a

No, you are an ambitious physicist who is hesitant.

4

You wonder if your comfort is related to physics.
You board a 100-year-old ship.

3a

No, you board a Chinese cargo ship

2a

No, your story begins with a Google Hangout
between yourself and a <u>ship spotter</u>
who tracks the movements of cargo ships around the

ST: pass script to audience member 4a.

1b: pass script to audience member 1c.

2a: pass script to audience member 2b.

world, including a Chinese cargo ship.

1b
No, you're watching the movements of
your friends and family and colleagues and neighbors.

2a
No, you're chasing after botanists on an island
in the middle of the Panama Canal.

4
No, you're voyaging through the Arctic Waters.
You go to the Arctic annually, before the ice forms.
Your boat freezes into place,
and you stay put until the ice thaws.

3b
You let us know this is called "overwintering,"
staying put through the severe conditions of winter.

1b
You watch majestic glaciers drift by
in all their mystery and wonder.

4a
You say, "I love this, or I'm good at this!"

2a
You know that, in 1953,
the confluence of a high spring tide,
a windstorm, and a tidal surge
caused massive flooding
and ultimately killed thousands of people.

3b: pass script to audience member 3c.

4a: pass script to audience member 4b.

1c: pass script to audience member 1d.

1c

You recognize that
an equally devastating weather event looks imminent,
only this time sea levels are higher,
much higher.

3b

You join the movement and try to solve the puzzle
with the help of a married couple.

4a

No, with the help of a cranky German artist
who dismally deliberates the ethics of the journey.

1c

When you describe how cold water would run southeast,
get pulled into the Atlantic Ocean, build, hit land
and possibly funnel up the estuary,
our response—after bewilderment—is epiphany.
You stand up.

2b

We plot an audacious action aimed at stealing the media
spotlight and driving real change.

3c

You wittily illustrate the obstacles to this action with a
fetching musical number.

4b

We film an interview with the cranky German artist.

1d

No, we film a group of physicists performing research on
the island.

2b: pass script to audience member 2c.

4b: pass script to audience member 4c.

1d: pass script to audience member 1e.

2b
No, we film our parents.

4b
We get up
and look out at magnificent bodies of water, glaciers,
landscapes that make us feel minuscule
in the grand scheme of things.

1d
We are tiny specks in this room, in the cosmos,
mortal creatures just fighting to survive.

3c
We say, "But this is thousands of miles from us."

2c
We say, "But this is <u>here</u>. Here we are."

3c
We recognize that we humans are expeditiously
taking nature down.

1e
No, we humans are rapidly taking ourselves down.

4c
We lay out the climate crisis in plain didactic terms.

2c
Here is what's happening.

1e
We have choices to make.

1e: pass script to audience member 1f.

4c: pass script to audience member 4d.

3c
Now is the time to make them.

4c
Sacrifice will be required.

1e
This is how we survive day to day.

2c
It's how we survive.

1e
It's how we move.

3c
We twist and turn toward a rather absurd culmination.

4c
We're dying to see how the mystery will be resolved.

2c
We are all standing up.

4c
We are closing the gap.

3d
We came. We sat. We ate. We ate dessert.

1f
All the humans gathering to examine each tiny moment.
All the humans gathering, each weighing in.

4d: pass script to audience member 4e.

2d: pass script to audience member 2e.

3d: pass script to audience member 3e.

1f: pass script to audience member 1g.

3d
We had to expect there to be some backlash from that.

4d
Which one is your favorite? I mean,
which one would you return to,
over and over again?

2d
Year after year? Decade after decade?

3d
Generation after generation?

1f
How many?

4e
"Certainty is now lost to us, whatever our politics."[6]

2e
"What we are really dealing with here
is akin to the original meaning of compassion."

3e
"It is inseparable from
the currents of matter, energy, and information
that flow through us and sustain us
as interconnected open systems."

1g
Like nose blowing.

4e
Like skirt pinning.

4e: pass script to audience member 4f.

3e: pass script to audience member 3f.

2e: pass script to audience member 2f.

1g
"We are not closed off from the world,
but rather are integral components of it,
like cells in a larger body."

3e
Time. Energy. Resources.

2e
Acknowledgment. Credit given.

4e
The reality of money that stares us down.

3e
The actual position of not having enough food to eat
or a healthy place to live.

1g
A state of mind.

2e
And a physical state.

4f
We're in a physical state.

3f
There is a springtime fullness.

2f
There is running in fields.

3f
Those smells like grass and floral blooms.

1g: pass script to audience member 1h.

4f: pass script to audience member 4g.

2f: pass script to audience member 2g.

3f: pass script to audience member 3g.

1g
General and specific.

4f
There is blood and movement and rush.

2f
An energy—zip zap pulse pulse pulse
Firing on all of those cylinders.

4f
Maximum capacity.

2f
Maximum output.

1h
I see it coming.

3f
I see spring back there, back there.

1h
I see spring ahead.

4g
Some kind of stillness at the center of it.

2g
I see it coming.

1h
This is what we do.

2g: pass script to audience member 2h.

3g: pass script to audience member 3h.

4g: pass script to audience member 4h.

2g
We see many things coming.

3g
This is what we do.

4g
I see it coming.

2g
This is what we do.

3g
We see many things coming.

4g
This is what we do.

1h
A process, pretty folds cascading.

3g
This is what we do.

4g
We try and sometimes it works.

1h
We help when we can and don't when we can't.

2h
Sometimes we help when we can't.

3h
Largely we look down and sometimes it works.

E: sitting. You are aging subtly, but rapidly. You get very old.

Settle in.

Question acceptance.

Acknowledge patience.

Acknowledge continuation.

1h

If it doesn't work, we work.

4g

If it doesn't work, sometimes we look another way.

3h

Largely we get up and then sometimes it works.
Sometimes we all get up.

2h

This is what we do.

E: toward the end of this section, quietly, begin this
*monologue. It continues for a while after **You/No** ends.*

E

You did more than any other human on this Earth
to demonstrate that our actions have led to
global-scale changes.
You always found the perfect turn of phrase,
language, image,
the perfect way of boiling down complex ideas.
This is what you did.
You kept your habits close to what we had established
over time: dinner in bed, me on the chair next to you,
talking about yesterday and tomorrow,
what we needed to do,
about people I know, people you love,
how you were feeling,
if you were capable of working, of seeing visitors,
or just staying in bed watching your favorite shows,
or reading.
Largely you looked up and sometimes it worked.
Often I would ask a question about

something unfolding,
to hear your perspective.
You were, as they say in Texas,
one long, tall drink of water.
Your slender stretch in a doorway,
your bashful grin before vocalizing some insight,
allegation, objection.
This is what you did.
You helped when you could.
Your voice was lucid and steady,
despite open hostility by forceful opponents—
those who seek to make laws according to
fantasy and fake news.
It was an honor to share inside jokes,
homecooked meals, and red wine.
You embodied courage.
This is what you did.
You were undaunted.
It was an honor to call you my collaborator and friend.
This is what we do.
The road that you chose—to wholly acknowledge
the interdisciplinary nature of the issue—was not easy.
Yet without you and your choice,
humankind would not be on the brink of change.
A process, pretty folds cascading.
We try and sometimes it works.
We help when we can and don't when we can't.
It was an honor to know your love,
your profound dedication.
This is what we do.
We try and sometimes it works.
We help when we can and don't when we can't.
Sometimes we help when we can't.
Largely we look up and then sometimes it works.
If it doesn't work, we work.

If it doesn't work, sometimes we look another way.
Largely we look down and sometimes it works.
This is what we do.
Sometimes we look another way.
Largely we look up and then sometimes it works.
Sometimes it doesn't work.
Sometimes we work.
This is what we do.
If it doesn't work, we go to work.
If it doesn't work, sometimes we look another way.
We help when we can and we don't when we can't.
Sometimes it is difficult to make up one's mind.
We do not always know what we do.
Largely we try and look and work.
If it doesn't work, sometimes we look another way.
Largely we try and look and work.
This is what we do.
Sometimes we help when we can't.
Sometimes it doesn't work.
Sometimes we don't work.
Largely we try and then sometimes it works.
We do not always know what we do.
Sometimes it is difficult to make up one's mind.
A process, pretty folds cascading.
If it doesn't work, sometimes we look another way.
We help when we can and we don't when we can't.
Sometimes we don't help when we can
and don't when we can't.
Sometimes we don't and can't
but sometimes we can and do or don't.
Largely we look up and then sometimes it works.
This is what we do.
Sometimes we can help when we don't.
Sometimes we can't help what we do.
If it doesn't work, sometimes we look another way.

Largely we look down and then sometimes it works.
Sometimes it is difficult to make up one's mind.
This is what we do.
Sometimes it doesn't work.
Sometimes we don't work.
Sometimes we don't when we can't.
If it doesn't work, sometimes we try another way.
We look when we can and we don't when we can't.
Sometimes we don't look when we can't.
Largely we try and sometimes it works.
This is what we do.
"It is the most supremely interesting moment in life,
the only one, in fact, when living seems life,
and I count in the greatest good fortune
to have these few months
so full of interest and instruction
in the knowledge of my approaching death.
It is as simple in one's own person
as any fact of nature,
the fall of a leaf
or the blooming of a rose,
and I have a delicious consciousness, ever present,
of wide spaces close at hand,
and whisperings of release in the air."[7]
A process, pretty folds cascading.
Coming in waves and droves and veins and trickles.
"This long slow dying is no doubt instructive,
it is disappointingly free from excitements…
One sloughs off the activities one by one,
and never knows that they're gone,
until one suddenly finds that the months have slipped
away and the sofa will never more be laid upon,
the morning paper read,
or the loss of the new book regretted."
This is what we do.

We look when we can and we don't when we can't.
Sometimes we help when we can't.
"Don't let the 'sound' of us reverberate
within your imagination…
It is all so natural and simple and nothing
comes to which we are not adequate…
Don't think of me simply as
a creature who might have been something else…
I have always had a significance for myself…
and what more can a human soul ask for?"
Largely we look up and then sometimes it works.
If it doesn't work, we work.
If it doesn't work, sometimes we try another way.
This is what we do.
Sometimes we look another way.
Largely we look down, and then sometimes it works.
Sometimes it doesn't work.
Sometimes we don't work.
This is what we do.
We see many things coming.
This is what we do.
A process, pretty folds cascading.
Coming in waves and droves and veins and trickles.
We try and help and sometimes it works.
Like nose blowing.
Like skirt pinning.
We love this, or we're good at this.
like televised news anchors
like two antique stores and a phone booth
wandering through fields of airports
remarking on the way things used to be
the woods, remember
Antarctica
outer space
it's all far away from here

notes

1   Text in "Knee Conversation" is collaged from Internet user comments in response to "Doctors Discover a New Knee Ligament," an article by Gretchen Reynolds for *The New York Times*, published November 13, 2013.

2   Text in "ST Gets Dressed" is collaged from anonymous audience comments on surveys following the premiere of *it's [all] highly personal*, another performance work by SuperGroup and Rachel Jendrzejewski, presented by the Walker Art Center at the Southern Theater in Minneapolis as part of Momentum: New Dance Works 2013.

3   Text in "You/No 1" was inspired by critical reviews of other contemporary performances dealing with the subject of climate change, including works by The Civilians, Cynthia Hopkins, and Steve Waters.

4   Quotes from "Working Through Environmental Despair" by Joanna Macy, published in *Ecopsychology: Restoring the Earth, Healing the Mind*, ed. Theodore Roszak, Mary E. Gomes, and Allen D. Kanner (San Francisco: Sierra Club Books, 1995). Used with permission from Joanna Macy.

5   Text in "You/No 2" was inspired by critical reviews of other contemporary performances dealing with the subject of climate change, including works by The Civilians, Cynthia Hopkins, and Steve Waters.

6   Quote from "Working Through Environmental Despair" by Joanna Macy, published in *Ecopsychology:*

Restoring the Earth, Healing the Mind, ed. Theodore Roszak, Mary E. Gomes, and Allen D. Kanner (San Francisco: Sierra Club Books, 1995). Used with permission from Joanna Macy.

7   Quotes from the diary and letters of Alice James in 1891-1892, the last two years of her life. Retrieved from *The Diary of Alice James*, ed. Leon Edel (Dodd, Mead, 1964) and *The Death and Letters of Alice James: Selected Correspondence*, ed. Ruth Yeazell (University of California Press, 1981).

POP SONG

150

151

me— di–ate per– i – meter and the
me-di-ate per-i-met-er and rea— cha–ble space a–round and

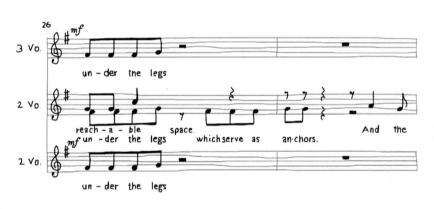

un— der the legs

reach – a – ble space which serve as an·chors. And the
un – der the legs

un – der the legs

un – der the legs

reach – a – ble space. which serve as an·chors. cresc _ _ _
un – der the legs

un – der the legs I love this

152

153

156

157

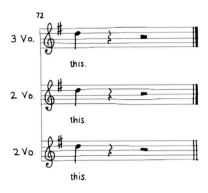

HOW WE SURVIVE

Sing in a relaxed conversational rhythm and tempo, with optional subtle changes of speed during the melismatic moments.

Notation Guide:
D = pitch value
/ = modulate up
\ = modulate down

D   D\C/D\C   \B
This is how we sur -   vive   day to day

\A   A/B/C\B
It's how we sur -   vive

\G   /B\A/B\A \F#   F#/G\E
Discover god by the   rail -   road   tracks

/B   \A   \F#/G/A/ /B   /C   \B
Understand   god as   hu -   man   con -   tact

B   /E   \B   /D   D\C\B/C   \B
The   ways   in which we   find   mea -   ning

\G   /A   /B\A/B/C /D
Like   nose   blow -   ing

D   \B   \A
Like shirt pin -   ning

\G   /D   \A   \G   /D   \B   \A
I love   this   or   I'm   good   at   this

A   A/B   B
Like televised news   an -   chors

\A   A/B   B   /C\B/C   \A
Like two an -   tique   stores and a   pho -   ne booth

\G   G\F#
Wandering through fields of air -   ports

160

```
\G                        /B          \A          \F#        F#/G\E
Remarking on the          way         things      used to    be


\D#
The woods


D#          /E          /F#         /G
Remem -     ber Ant -    arc -       tica


/A          /B          /C\B
Out -       er -        space


B           /E          \D#         /E\B/C\A  B         G           F#
It's        all far     a -         wa -      y         from        here
```

RACHEL JENDRZEJEWSKI is a writer and interdisciplinary artist who works throughout the U.S. and internationally, most often investigating awareness, embodied experience, and the complexities of "community." She frequently collaborates with dancers, visual artists, musicians, fellow writers, and alleged non-artists to explore new performative vocabularies. Her projects have been developed and/or presented by the Walker Art Center, Red Eye Theater, Public Functionary, Padua Playwrights, Joe's Pub at The Public Theater, The Wild Project, A.R.T., and ICA/Boston, among others. Other published plays include *encyclopedia* (Spout Press) and *Amber* (in the anthology *I Might Be the Person You Are Talking To: Short Plays from the Los Angeles Underground*, Padua Playwrights Press). Honors include a Playwrights' Center McKnight Fellowship, Core Writer Residency, and Jerome Fellowship; residencies at the University of Minnesota Institute for Advanced Study and MASS MoCA; and grants from the Minnesota State Arts Board, Network of Ensemble Theaters, and Foundation for Contemporary Arts. MFA Playwriting, Brown University. rachelka.com

SUPERGROUP is the Minneapolis-based performance collaboration of Erin Search-Wells, Sam Johnson, and Jeffrey Wells. Since forming in 2007, SuperGroup has created a variety of performance work, including full-evening dance / theater pieces, durational encounters in public spaces, and short queer cabaret performances across the Twin Cities and nationally. SuperGroup's work has been supported through commissions from the Walker Art Center, Red Eye Theater, and the Southern Theater, and grants from the Jerome Foundation, the Metropolitan Regional Arts Council, and the Minnesota State Arts Board. They received a McKnight Choreography Fellowship in 2017. As independent artists, the three members of SuperGroup perform, write, direct, choreograph, teach, and design in many performance permutations. supergroupshow.biz

acknowledgments

Special thanks to Jackie Beckey, Mike Bishop, Crystal Brinkman, Taylor Carik, Tyler Crumrine, Galen David, Angharad Davies, Hanlyn Davies, Heidi Eckwall, Erik Ehn, Hannah Geil-Neufeld, Laura Gisler, Theo Goodell, Miguel Gutierrez, Tricia Heuring, Kate Iverson, Amy and Andrew Jendrzejewski, Nancy Johnson, Joe and Jen Photography, Hannah Kramer, Les and Colleen Kramer, Alex Lange, Eric Larson, Kimberly Lesik, Joanna Macy, David and Iris Malley, Megan Mayer, Liz Miller, Crystal Myslajek, Lara Nielsen, Debra Orenstein, Jan Search, Kevin Springer, Stephanie Stoumbelis, Anne Symens-Bucher, Jeff and Jo Wells, Tom Wells, Abigail Zimmer, and the many thoughtful individuals who provided feedback and support throughout this work's development.